AUTHENTIC ART DECO JEWELRY DESIGNS

837 Illustrations

EDITED BY FRANCO DEBONI

ARRANGED BY THEODORE MENTEN

Dover Publications, Inc., New York

Publisher's Note

The term "Art Deco" is derived from L'Exposition Internationale des Arts Décoratifs et Industriels Modernes, the exhibition held in Paris in 1925. It was there that the style, which had begun its evolution in the teens, was given worldwide attention and became a dominant force in design that flourished through the thirties.

Distinguished by its geometric and prismatic character, Art Deco was especially well suited for jewelry design; fine examples executed in the style are now greatly treasured and serve as inspiration for many modern pieces. The revival of interest should make all the more welcome this anthology, reproduced from an extremely rare—possibly unique—portfolio, probably of French or German origin. The range it covers is exceptionally wide, both in type of ornament and in treatment, the whole rendered with the jeweler's precision. Brooches, clasps, pins, studs, rings, bracelets, watches, necklaces, pendants, cigarette cases and lighters are depicted in designs revealing the full versatility and frequent wit of Art Deco.

Copyright © 1982 by Dover Publications, Inc.
All rights reserved under Pan American and International Copyright Conventions.

Published in Canada by General Publishing Company, Ltd., 30 Lesmill Road, Don Mills, Toronto, Ontario.

Manufactured in the United States of America
Dover Publications, Inc., 31 East 2nd Street, Mineola, N.Y. 11501

Library of Congress Cataloging in Publication Data
Main entry under title:

Authentic art deco jewelry designs.

1. Jewelry—History—20th century—Pictorial works.   2. Art deco—Pictorial works.
I. Deboni, Franco.
NK4710.3.A78A9   1982   739.27'022'2   82-9615
ISBN 0-486-24346-X (pbk.)

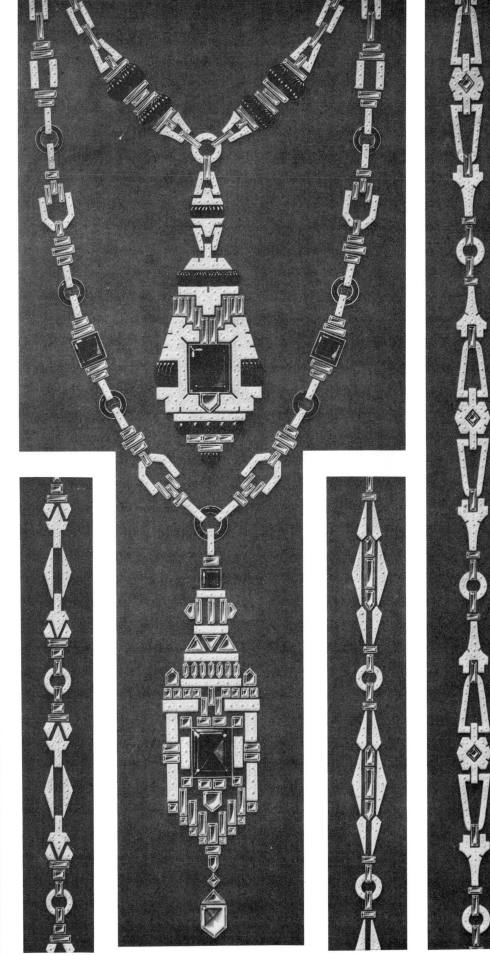

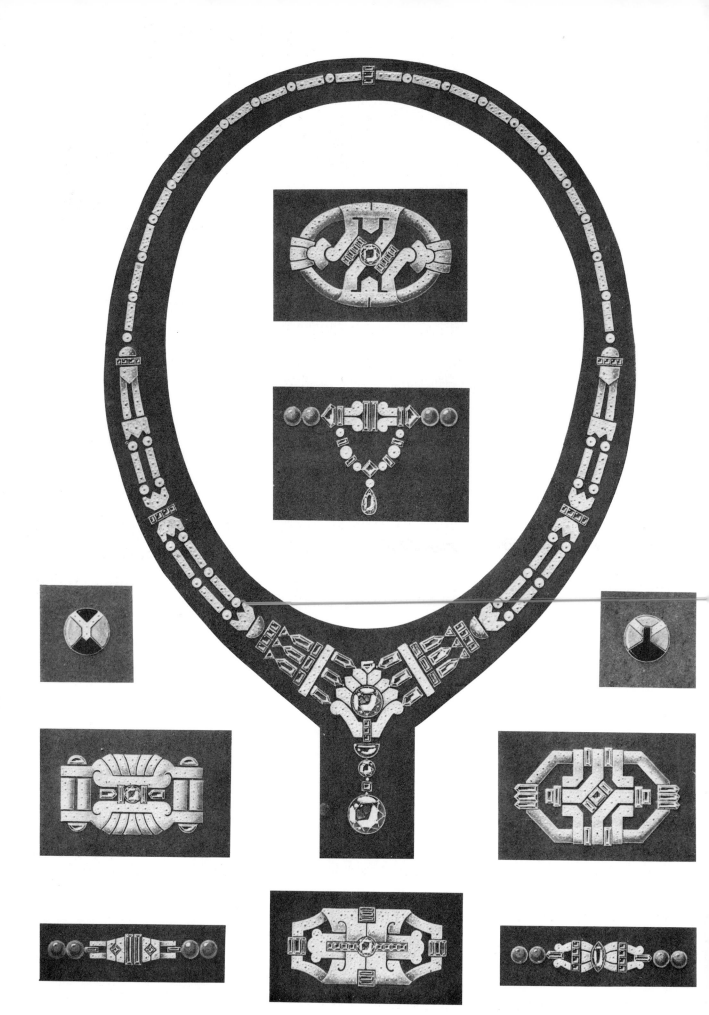

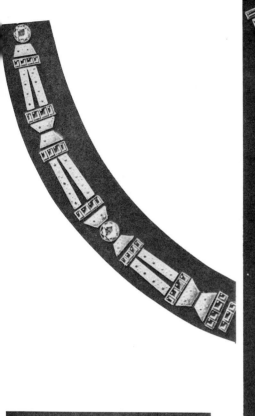

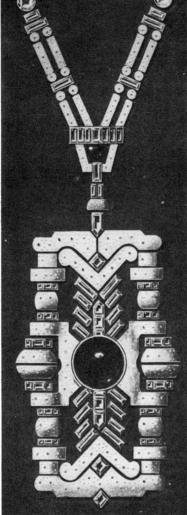

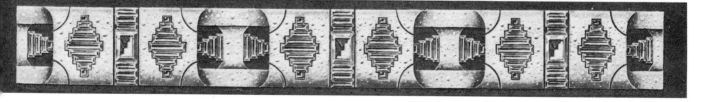

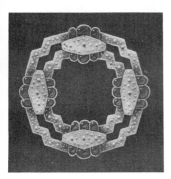

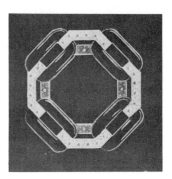

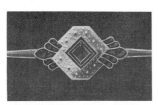

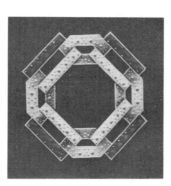

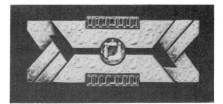

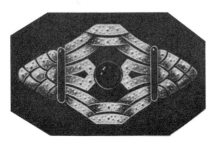

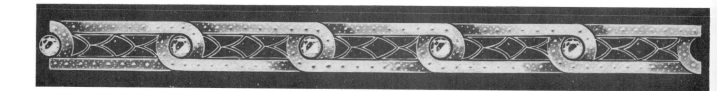

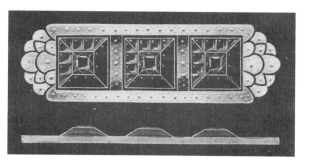

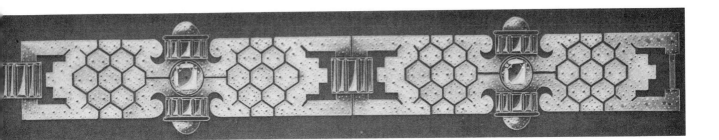

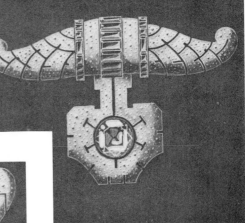

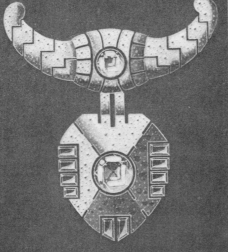

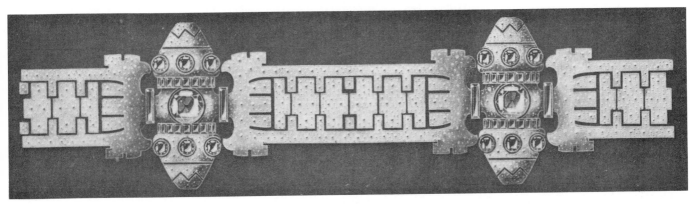

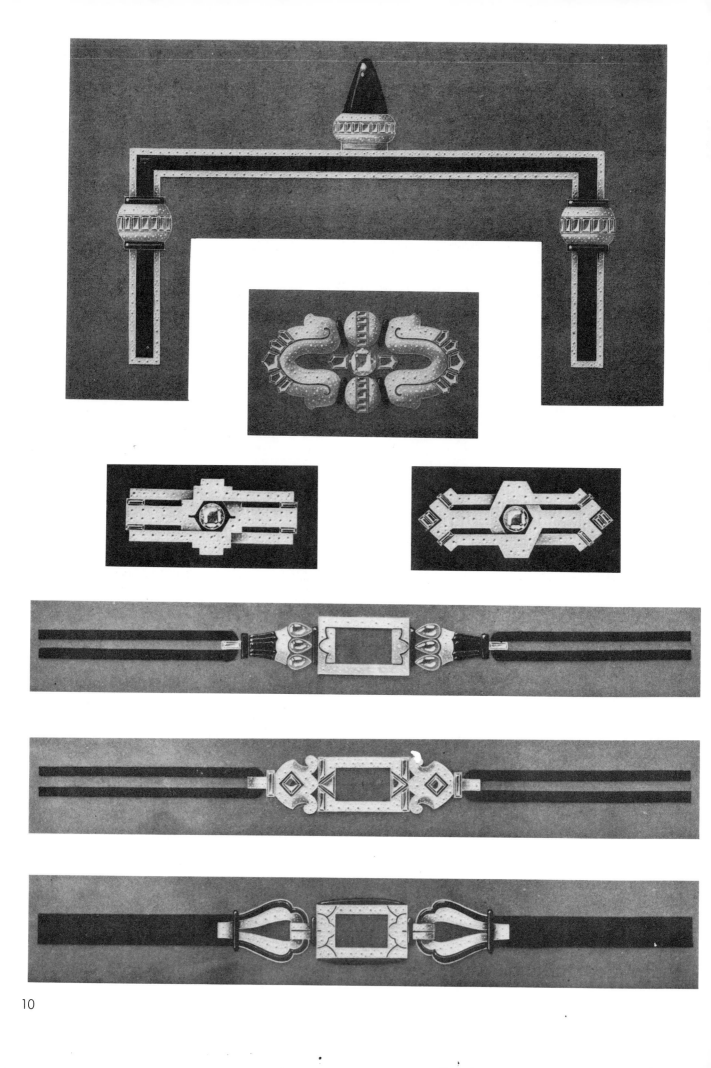

  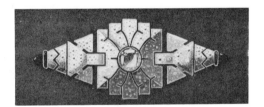

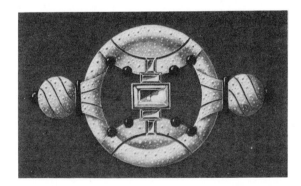 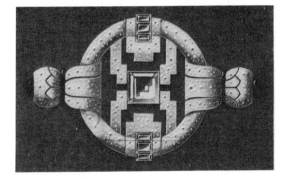

 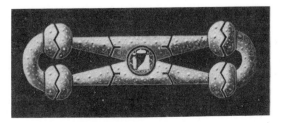

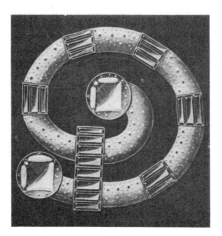

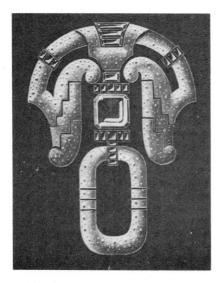

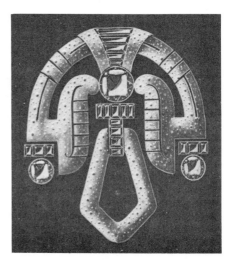

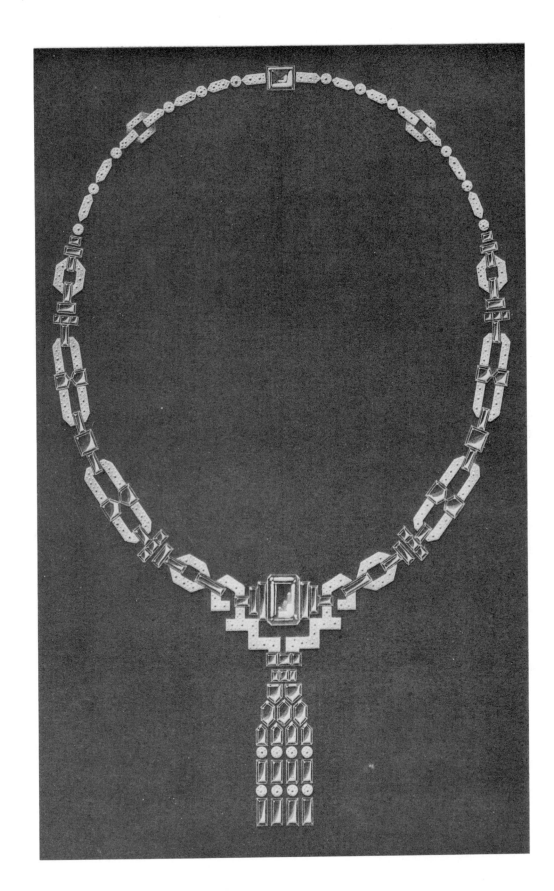

13

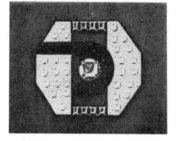

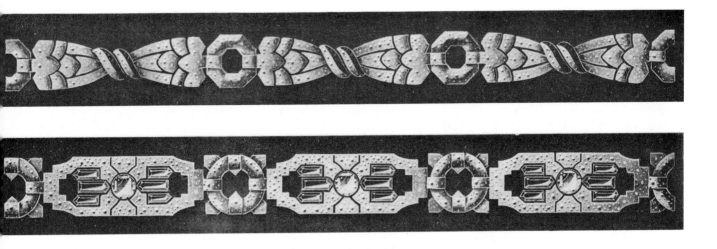

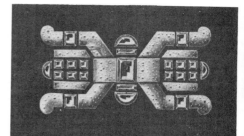
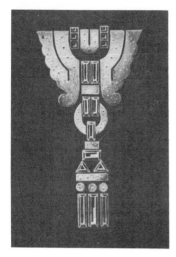

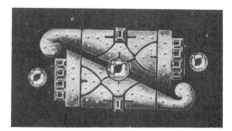

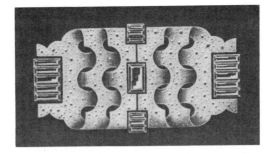
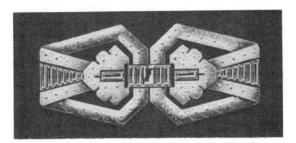

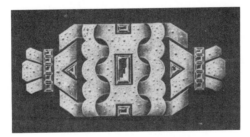
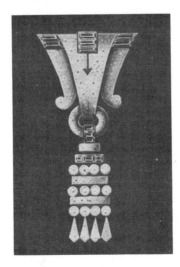

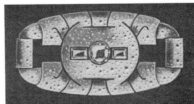

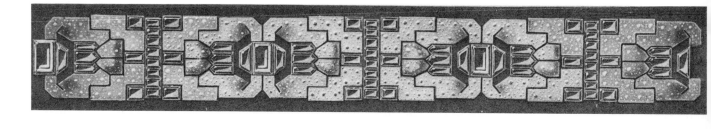

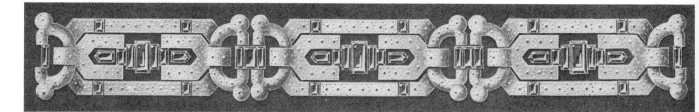

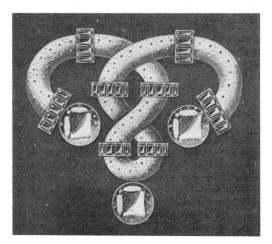

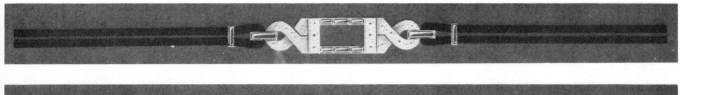

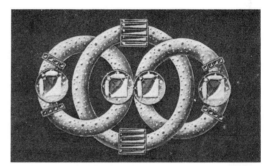

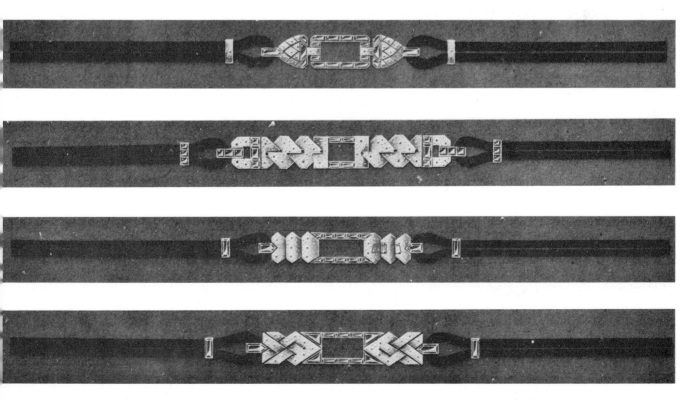

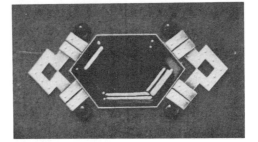

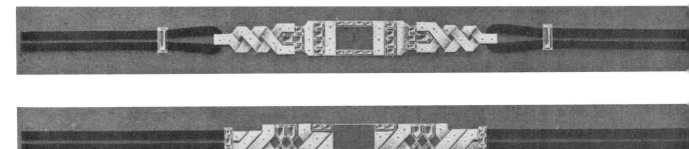

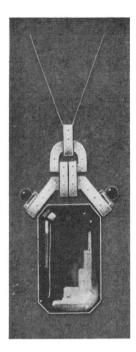

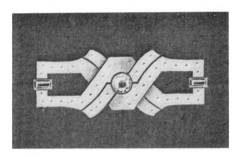

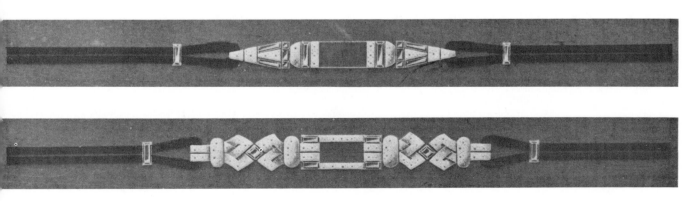

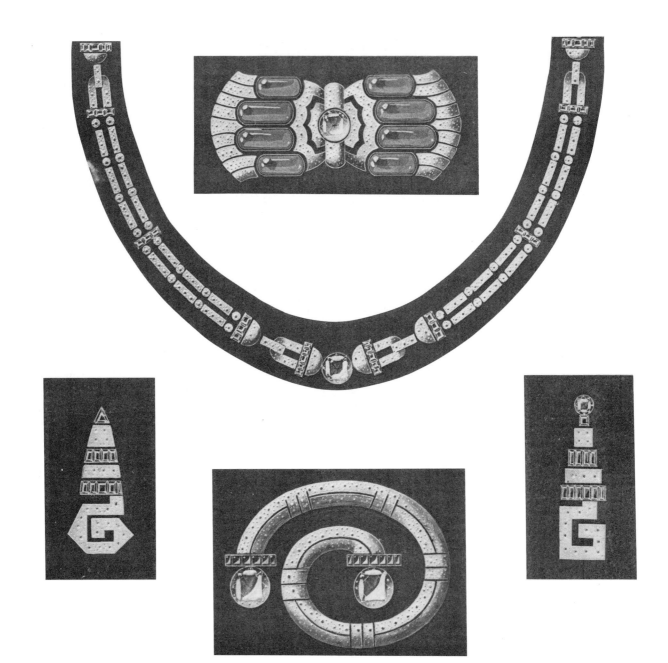

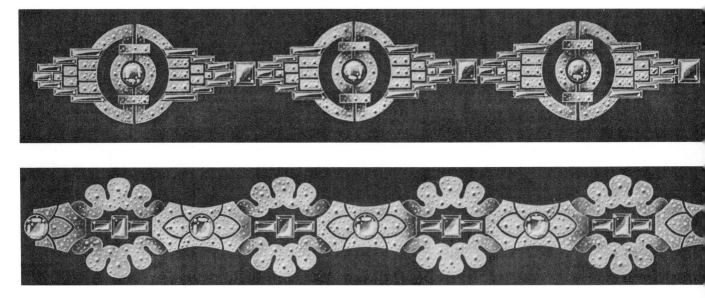

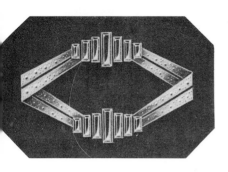

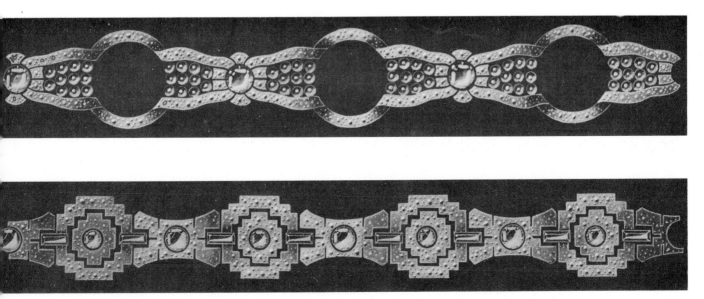

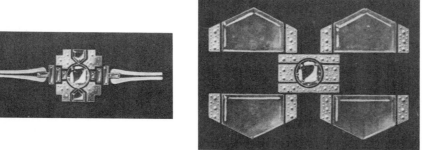

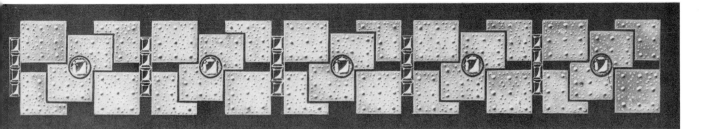

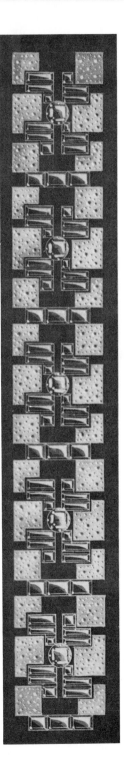

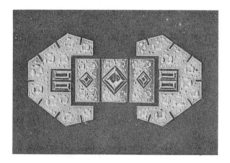

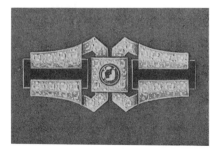

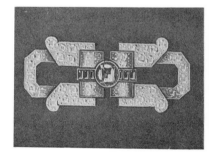

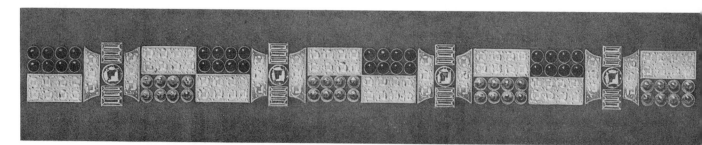

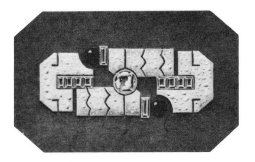

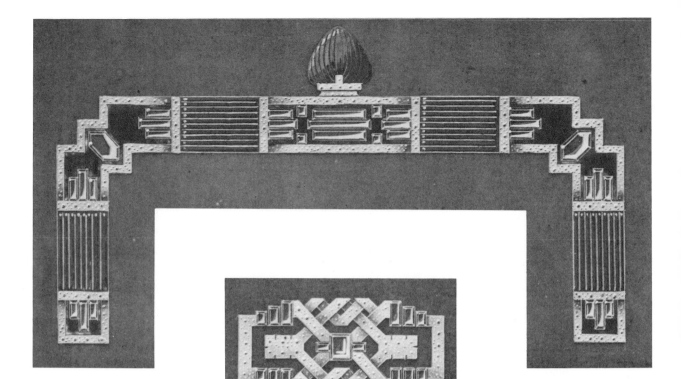

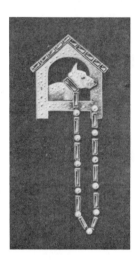
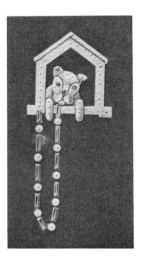

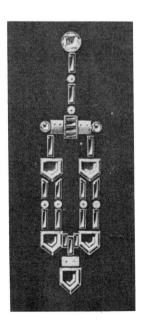

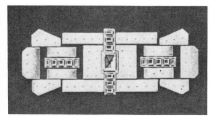

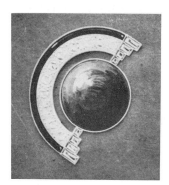

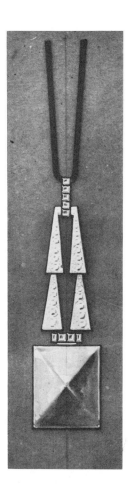

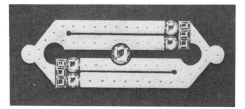

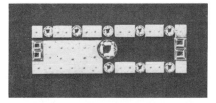

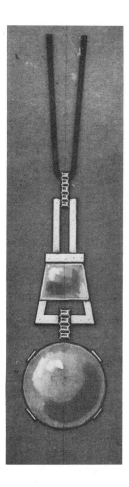

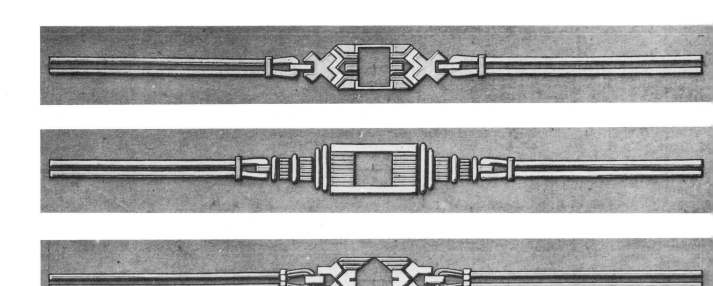

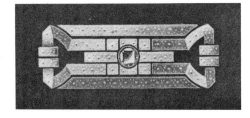

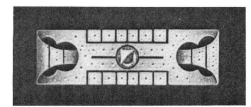

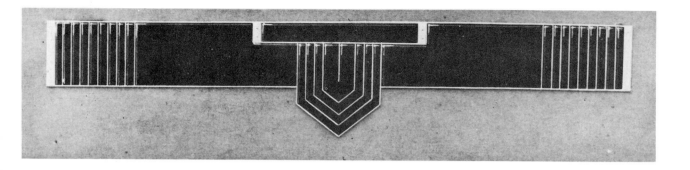

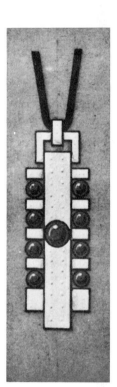

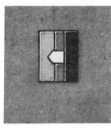

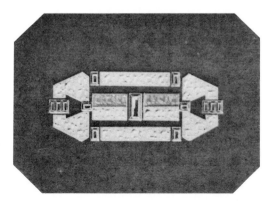

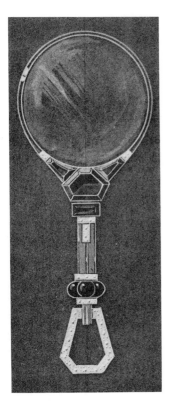

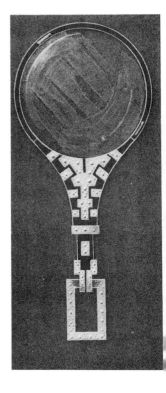

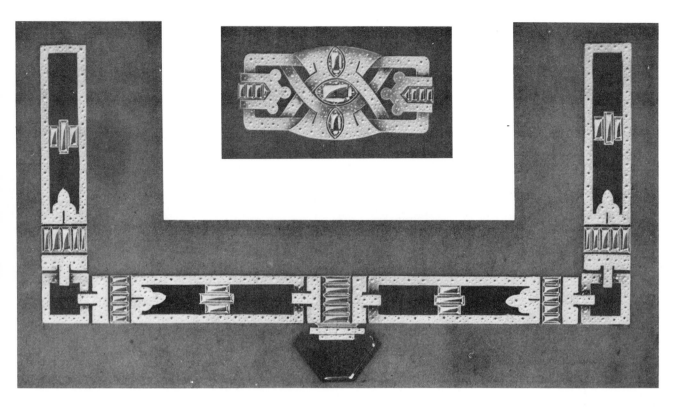

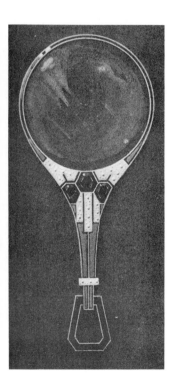

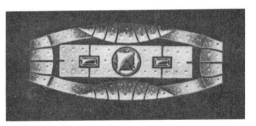

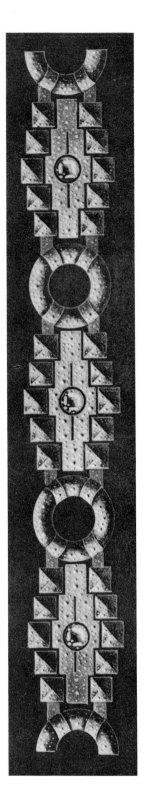
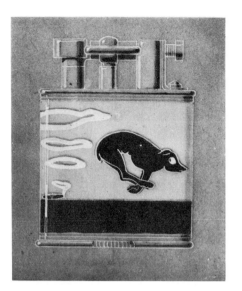

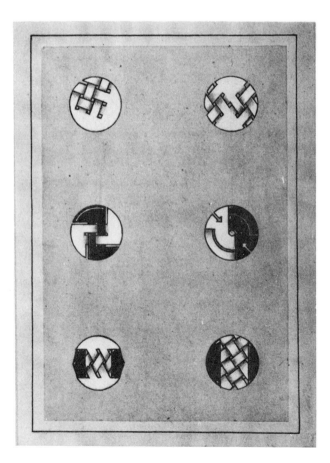

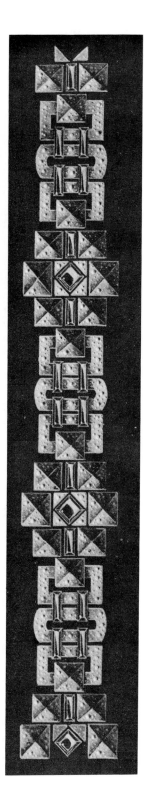

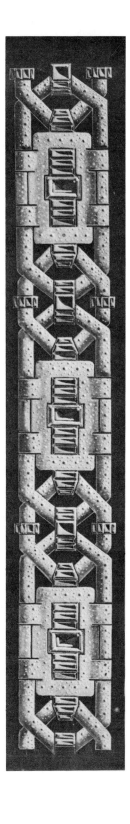

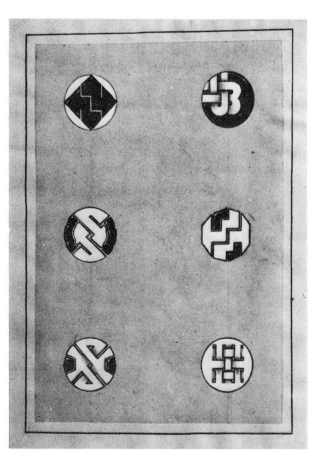

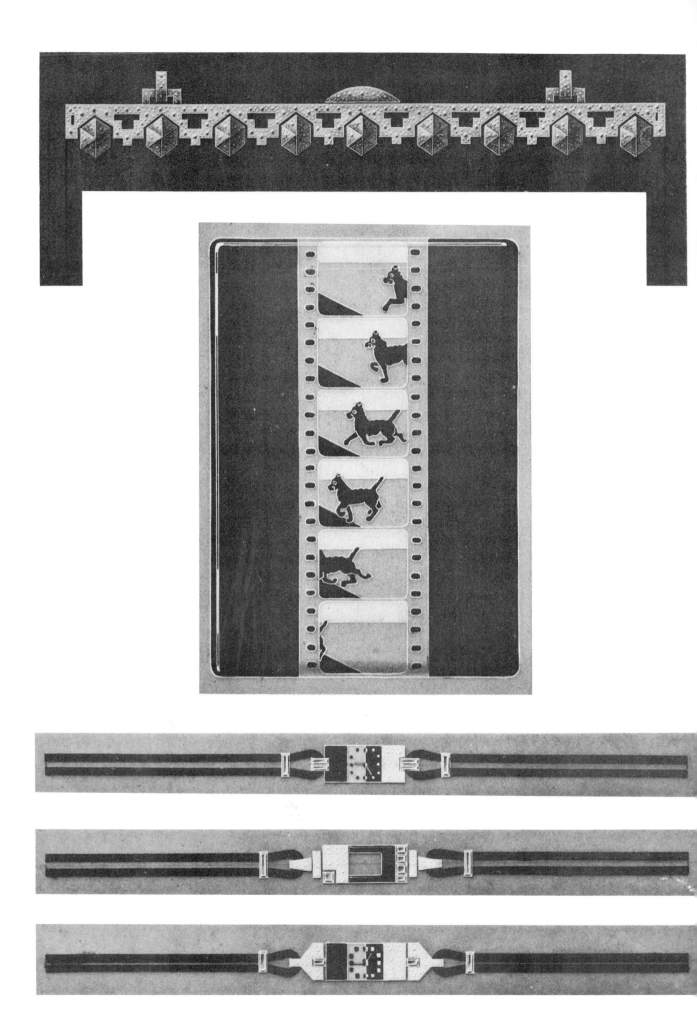

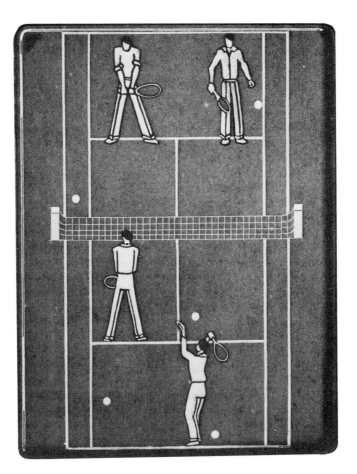

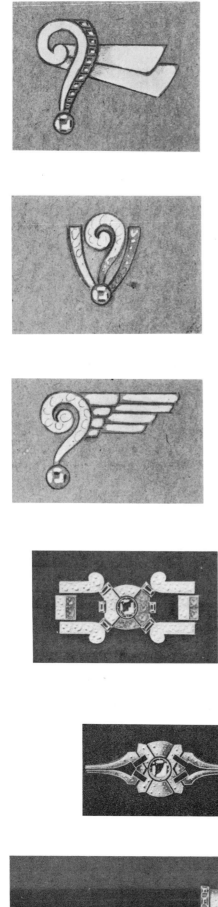

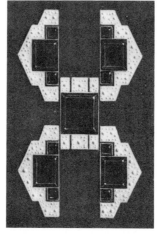

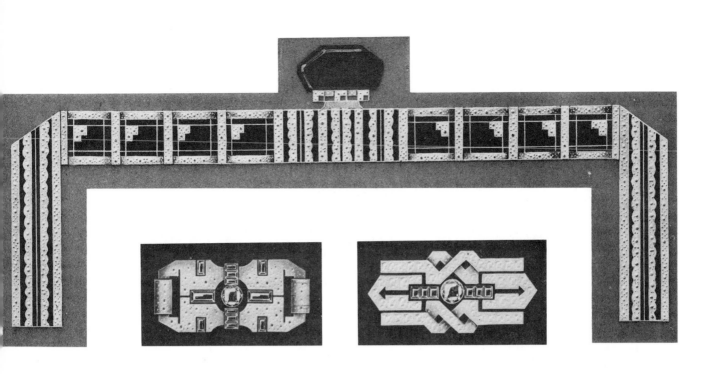

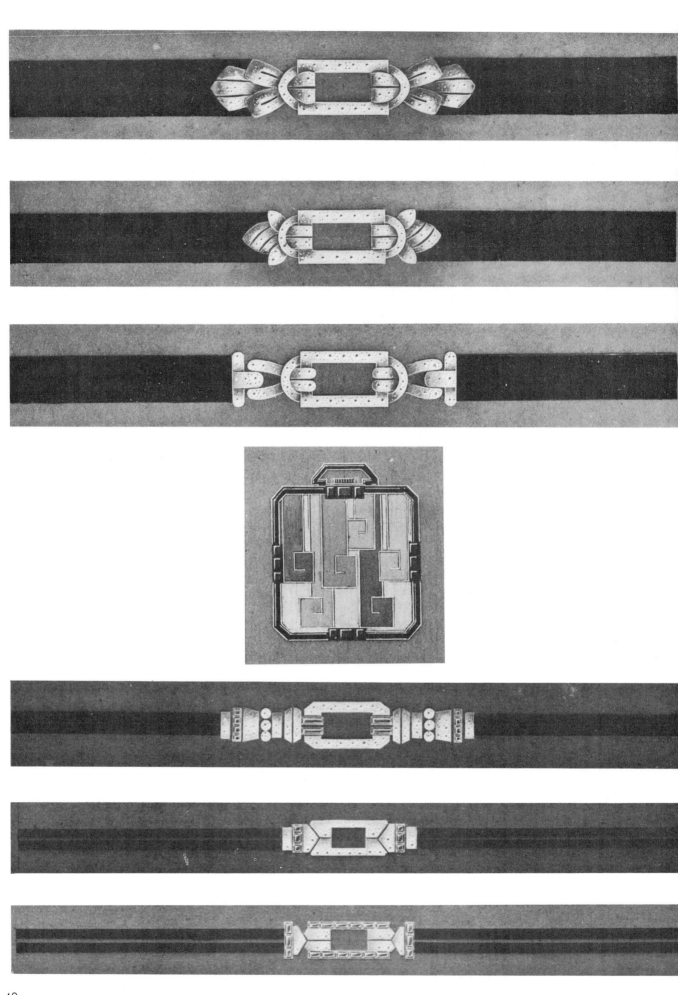

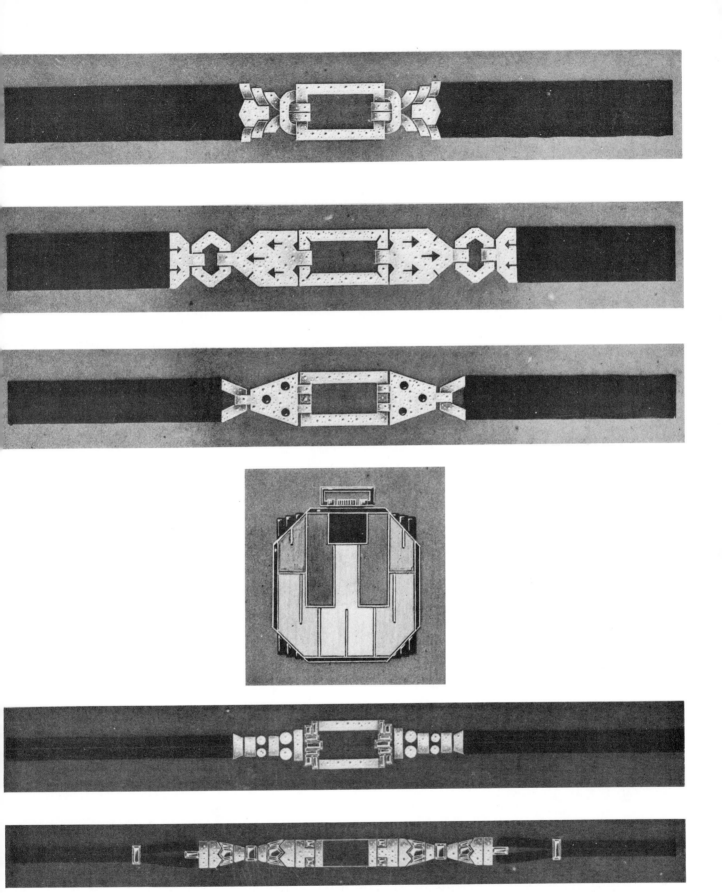

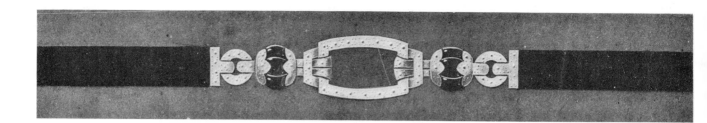

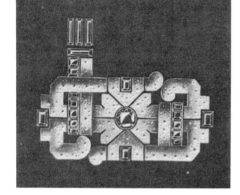

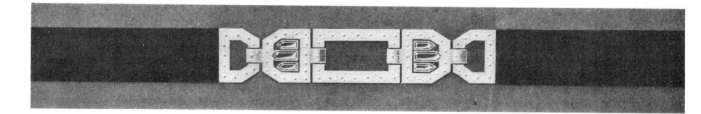

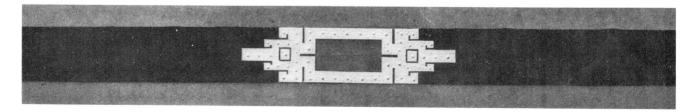

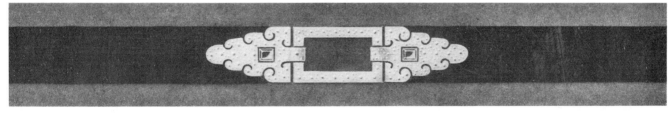

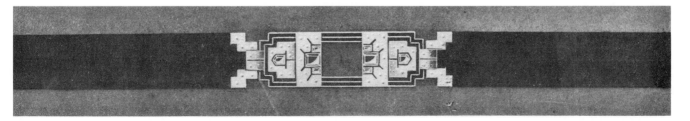

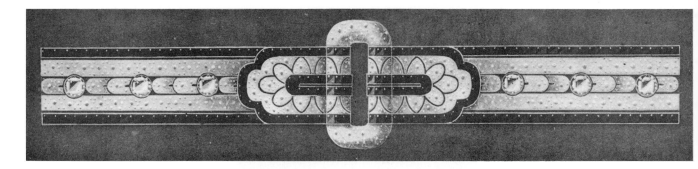

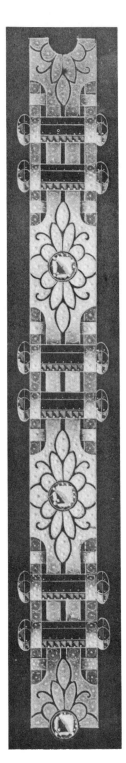

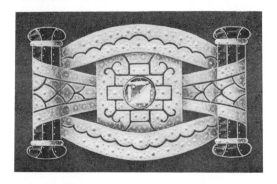

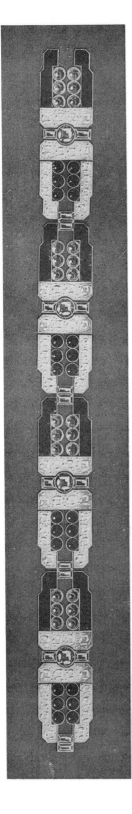

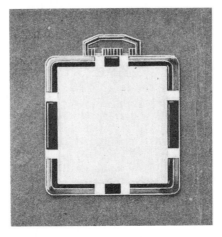

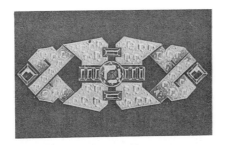

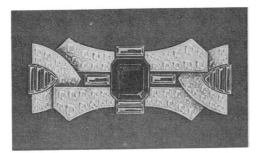

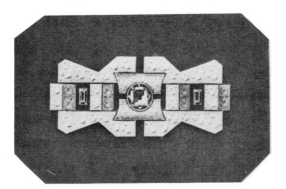

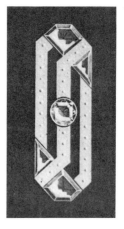

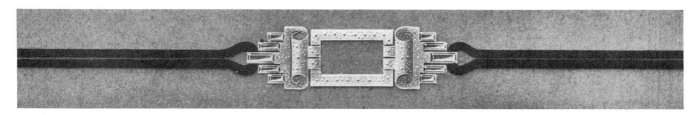

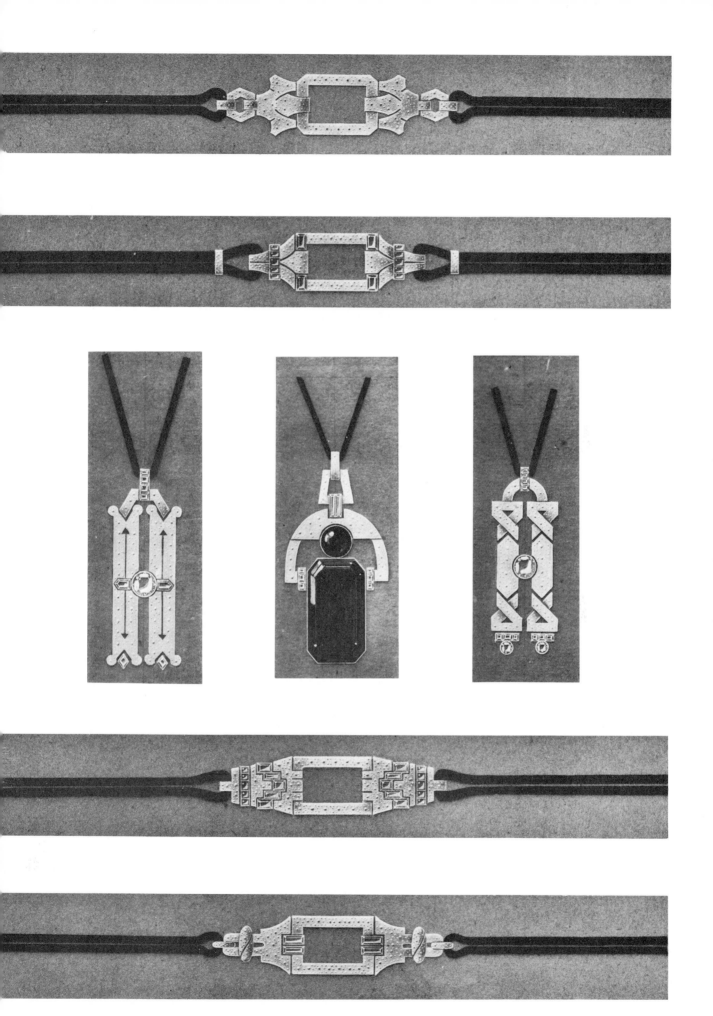

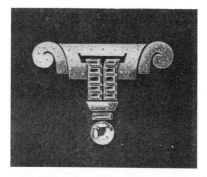

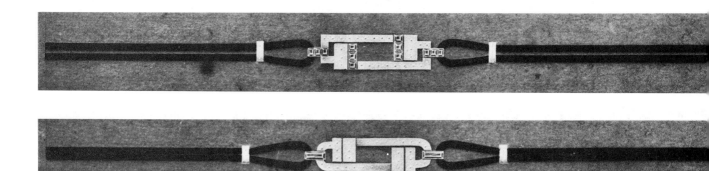

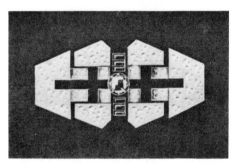

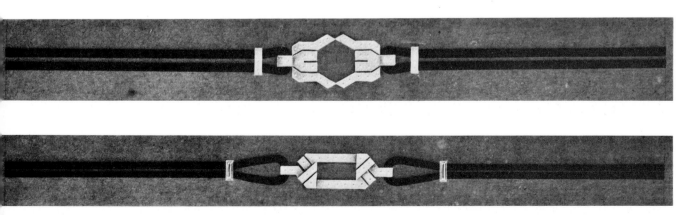

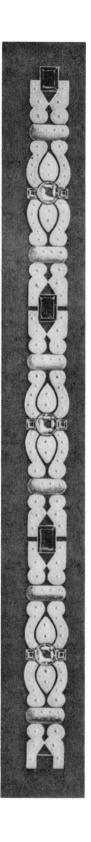

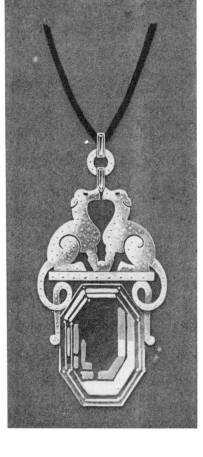

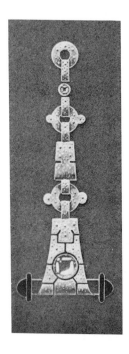

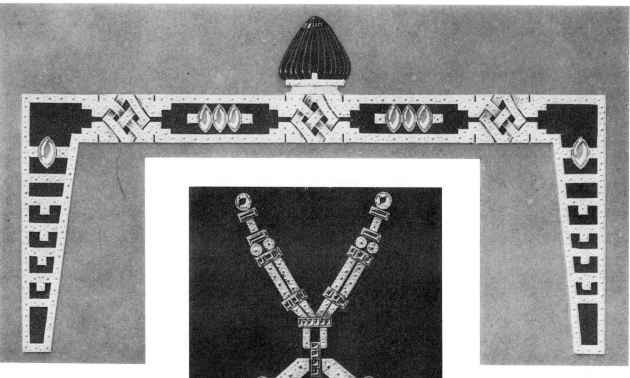

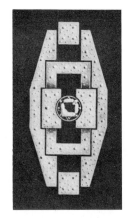
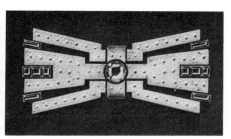
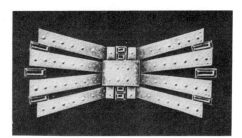

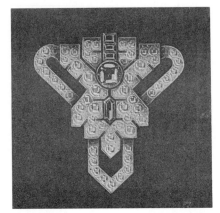

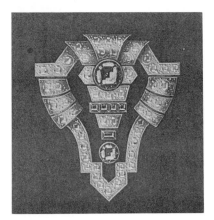

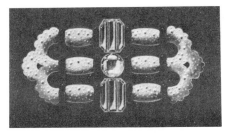

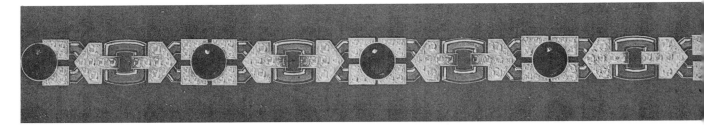

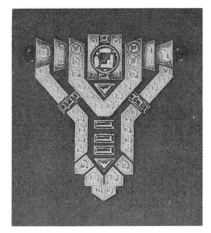

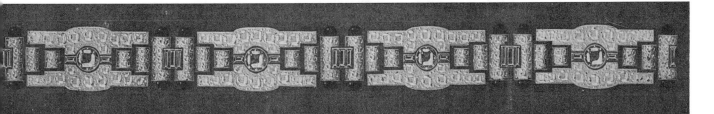

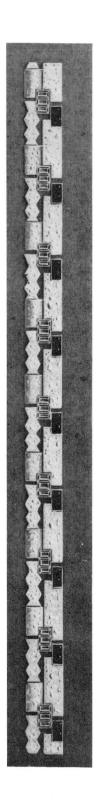

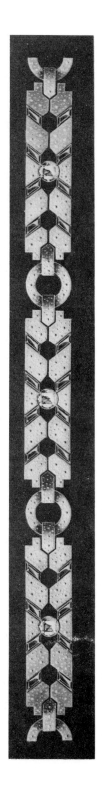

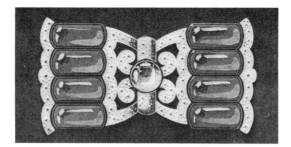

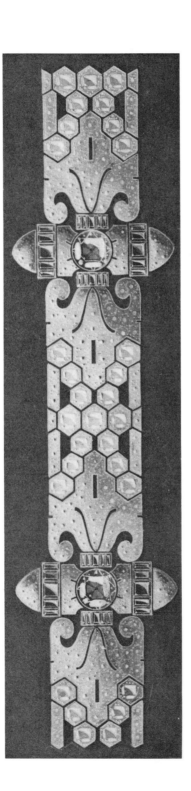

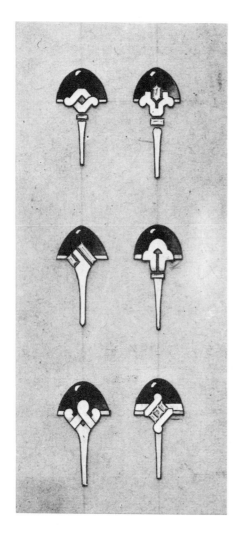

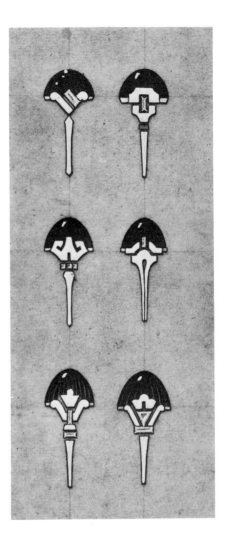

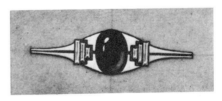

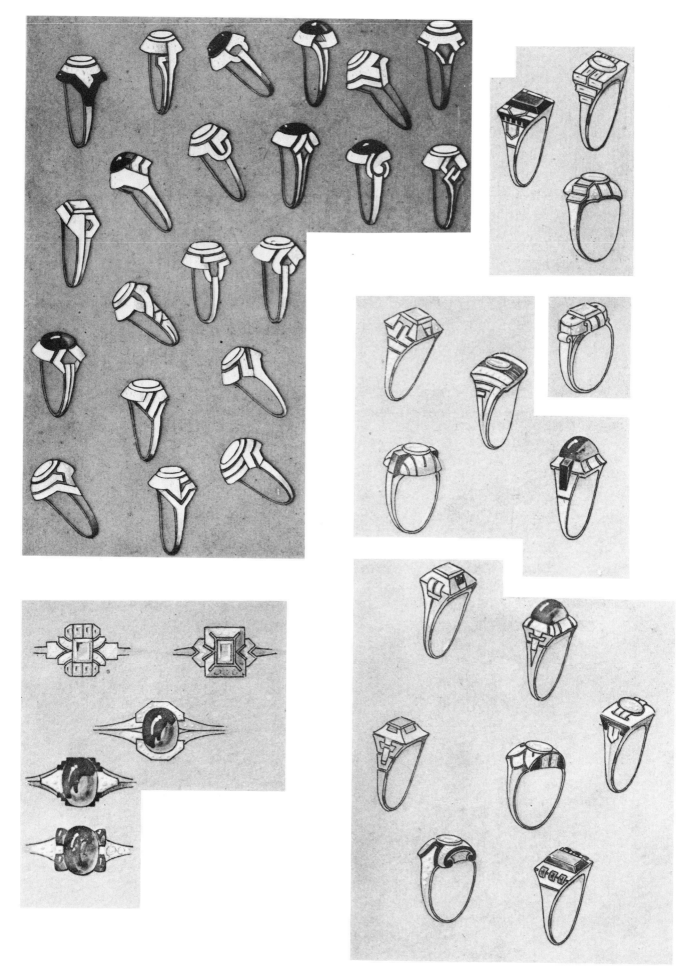

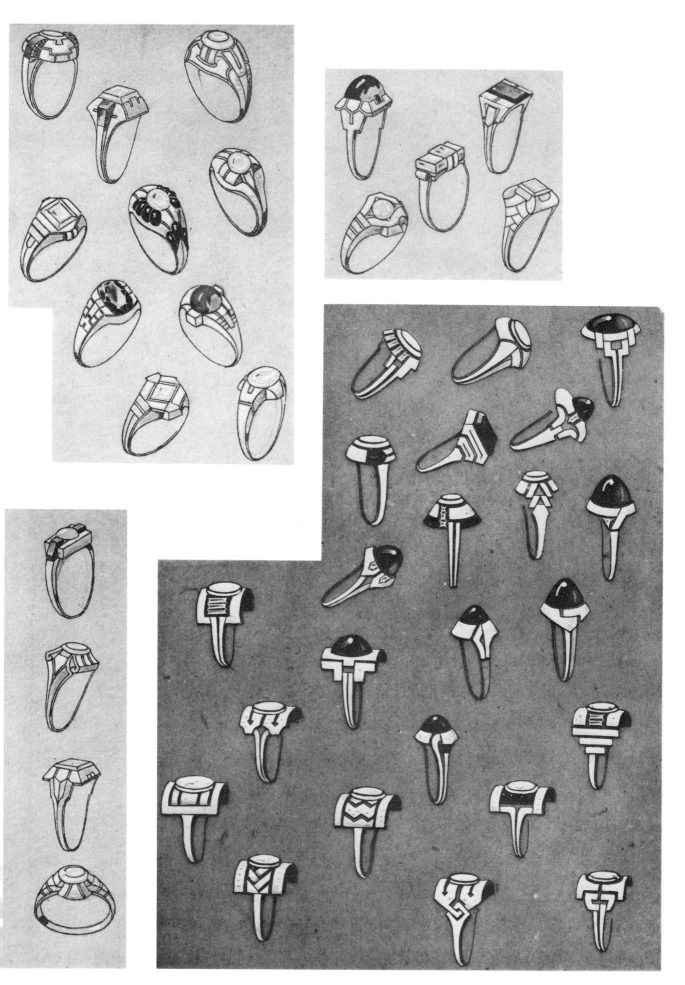

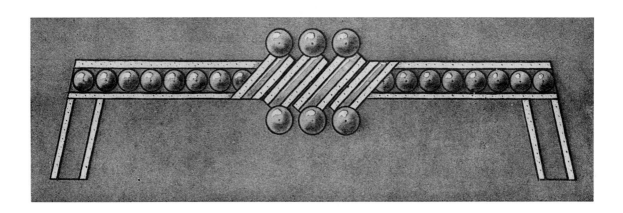

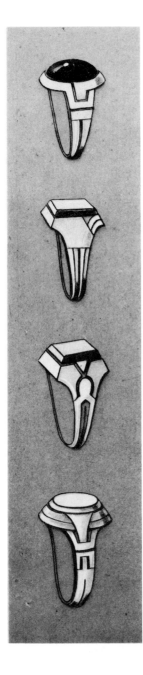

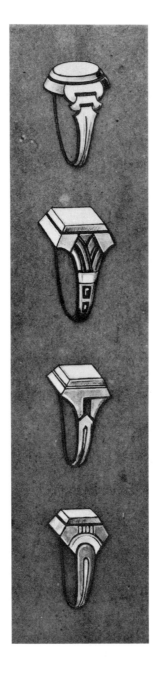

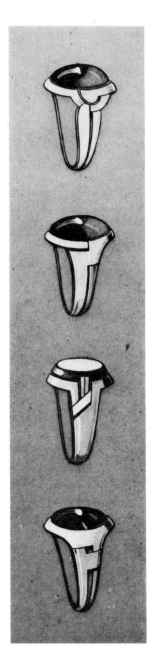

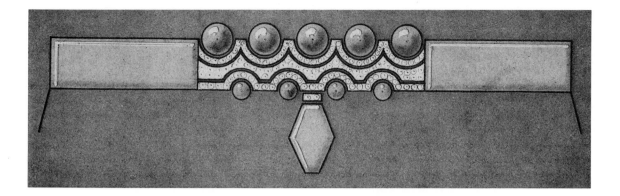

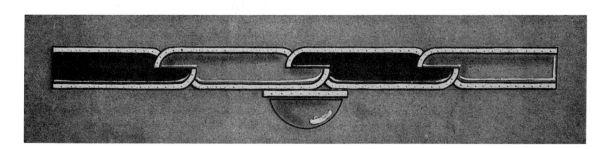

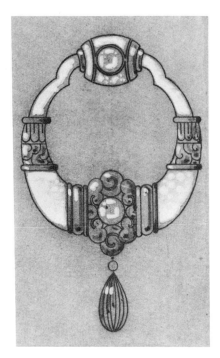

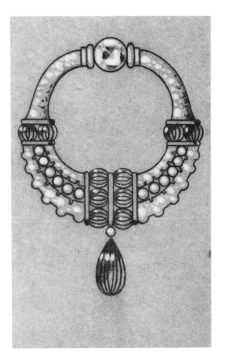

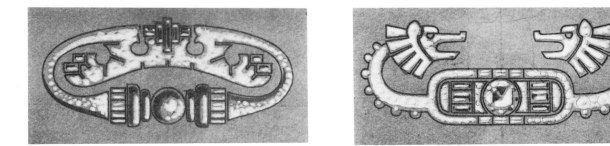

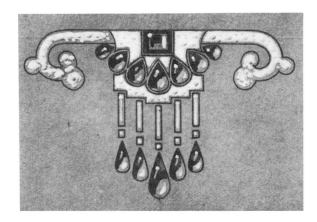

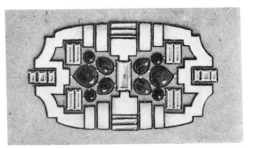

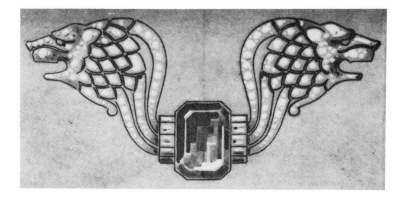

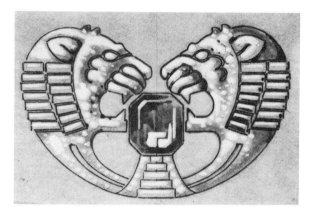

67

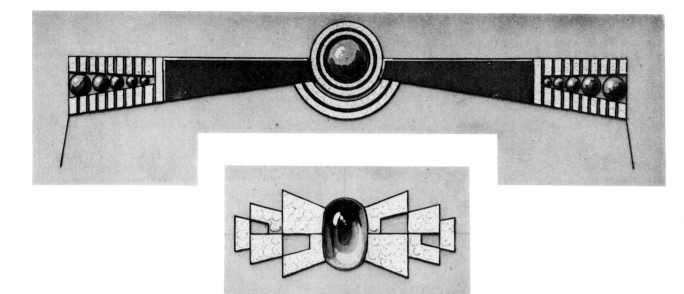

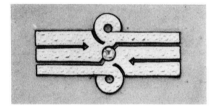 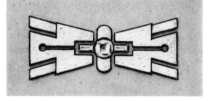 

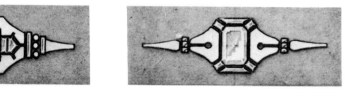

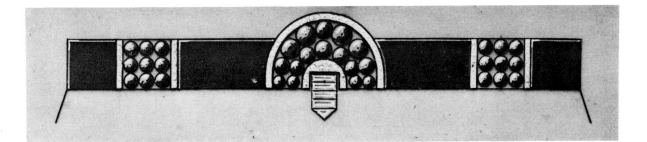

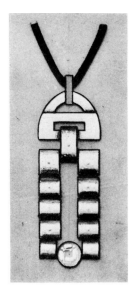

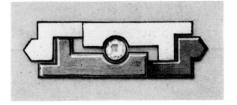

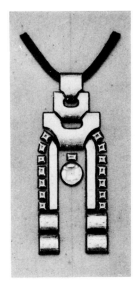

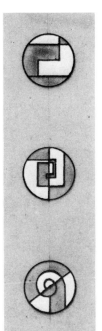

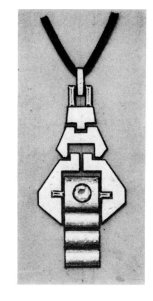

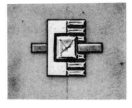

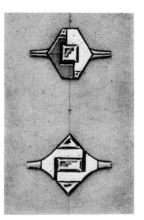

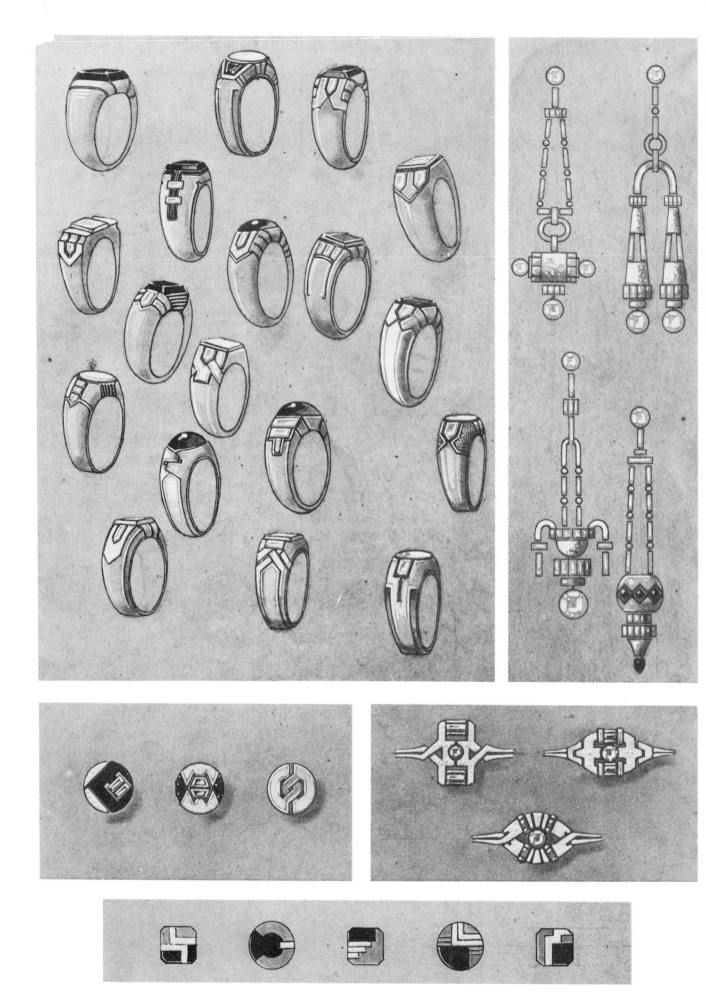

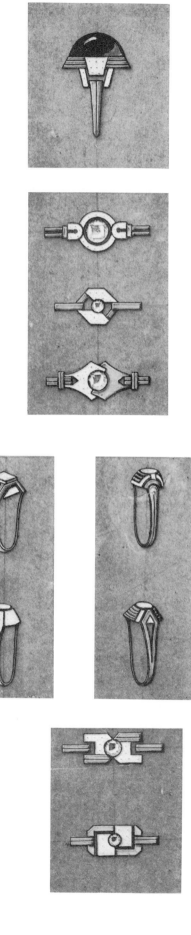

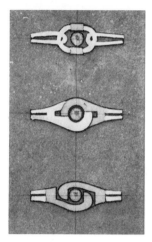

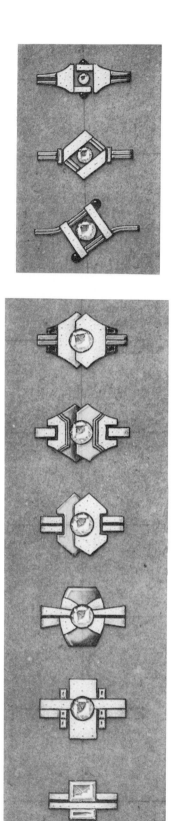

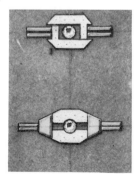

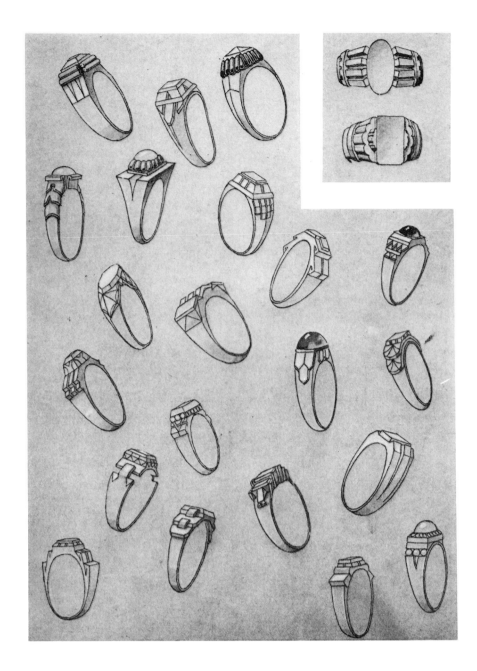

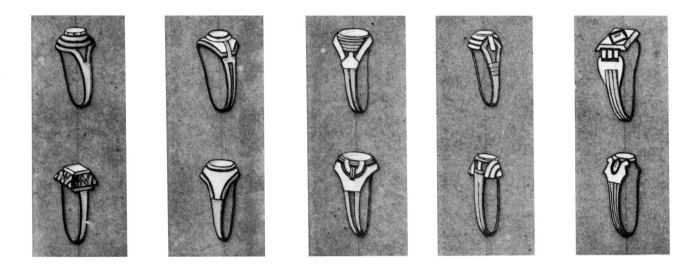

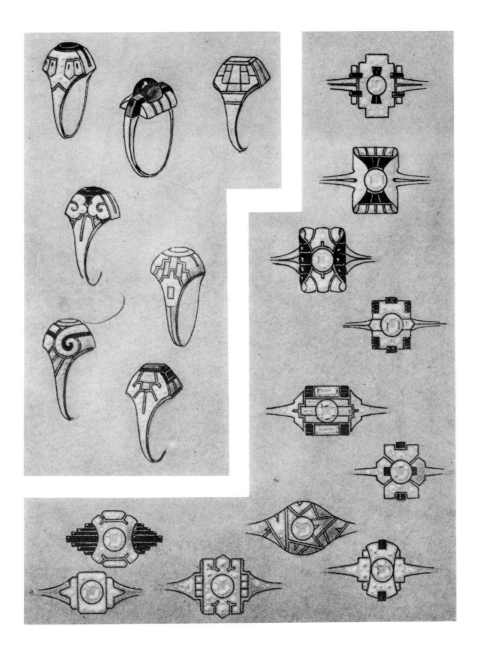

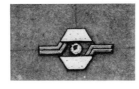

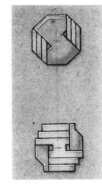
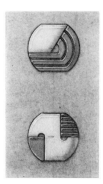

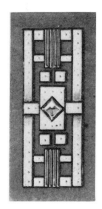

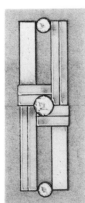
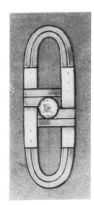

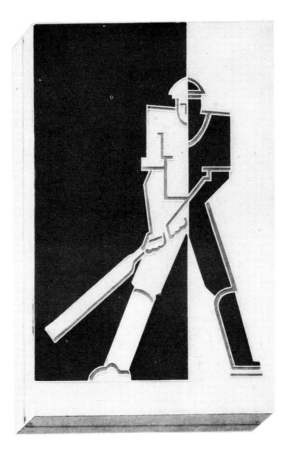

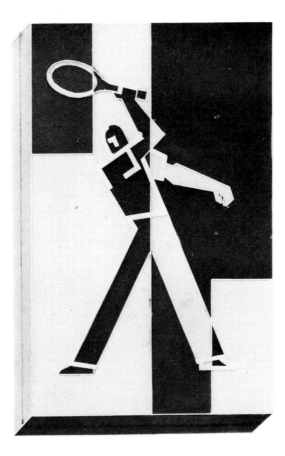